Sabine Picout

Doris Lessings "The Golden Notebook"

GRIN Verlag

Bibliografische Information der Deutschen Nationalbibliothek:

Die Deutsche Bibliothek verzeichnet diese Publikation in der Deutschen National-
bibliografie; detaillierte bibliografische Daten sind im Internet über http://dnb.d-
nb.de/ abrufbar.

Imprint:

Copyright © 2004 GRIN Verlag GmbH
Druck und Bindung: Books on Demand GmbH, Norderstedt Germany
ISBN: 978-3-656-09900-0

This book at GRIN:

http://www.grin.com/en/e-book/185054/doris-lessings-the-golden-notebook

GRIN - Your knowledge has value

Der GRIN Verlag publiziert seit 1998 wissenschaftliche Arbeiten von Studenten, Hochschullehrern und anderen Akademikern als eBook und gedrucktes Buch. Die Verlagswebsite www.grin.com ist die ideale Plattform zur Veröffentlichung von Hausarbeiten, Abschlussarbeiten, wissenschaftlichen Aufsätzen, Dissertationen und Fachbüchern.

Visit us on the internet:

http://www.grin.com/

http://www.facebook.com/grincom

http://www.twitter.com/grin_com

The Golden Notebook by Doris Lessing:

The Golden Notebook was published in 1962 and is one of the best known of Doris Lessing's novels.[1]

First I am going to give a short summary of *The Golden Notebook*. Then I want to explain the socio-political context of the book. This is the background of the novel itself and at the same time nearly identically to its main ideas. Afterwards I am going to analyse the structure of the work which again is closely connected to its interpretation. When I mention the most important characters you can follow my explanations on the sociogram which is in the handout. Because of the time limit, it is not possible to make more detailed explanations during my presentation

Now the short summary.

The central figure of *The Golden Notebook* is Anna Wulf, a writer from South Africa, living in London. During World War II Anna married a German refugee Max but divorce and then emigrate to London with her daughter Janet. She has a long love affair with Michael and an intense friendship with Molly.

Being about thirty Anna is in a life crises, disillusioned by communist politics under Stalin, doubting herself and her literary career. Therefore she needs the treatment of a psychotherapist. To get things straightened out with herself she deals them in four independent notebooks, each one has a different colour.

Socio-political context and main ideas:

As the following part will prove, *The Golden Notebook* shows features of a political novel as well as characteristics of a novel of ideas and has, besides this, various autobiographic traces.[2]

Racism is not a central topic in *The Golden Notebook* but the problem is mentioned when the protagonist, Anna, talks about her successful novel "Frontiers of War" which concerns race relations and forbidden love in southern Africa.[3]

Doris Lessing – herself growing up on a farm in Rhodesia – experienced racism and developed like Anna a strong resistance towards suppression and exploitation of the black natives.[4]

---

[1] Cf. Fahim, S. Shadia: Doris Lessing. Sufi Equilibrium and the Form of the Novel. St. Martin's Press, New York, 1994, p.51

[2] Cf. Lessing, Doris: The Golden Notebook. Paladin Grafton Books, London Glasgow, 1990, p. 13f. and Cf. Cheng, Yuan-Jung: Heralds of the Postmodern. Madness and Fiction in Conrad, Woolf, and Lessing. Peter Lang, New York, 1999, p. 76

[3] Cf. Fahim, S. Shadia: Doris Lessing, p. 53ff

[4] Cf. Stern, Frederick C.: Politics and The Golden Notebook. In: Kaplan, Carey/Rose, Ellen Cronan: Approaches to Teaching Lessing's The Golden Notebook. The Modern Language Association of America, New York, 1989, p. 37f.

Doris Lessing escaped from this colonial society to London like Anna. There she was confronted with the effects of the Cold War in the 1950s ‚which are mentioned in the novel just as the dangers of nuclear threats are.

Doris Lessing and Anna were both deeply involved in **politics** and together with most of their friends they became members of the Communist Party. But trials and atrocities in the Soviet Union and other communist countries or revelations about Stalin's crimes made them develop a feeling of doubt and disappointment towards Communism which was why they broke with communism.[5]

Besides this *The Golden Notebook* is about **feminism**. Although Lessing herself claimed in the preface to the book: "This novel was not a trumpet for Women's Liberation."[6] her friends called it "a tract about the sex war"[7].[8]

Anna and Doris Lessing being divorced with a child symbolize "a completely new type of woman"[9] because they "lead what is known as free lives, that is, lives like men,.."[10].

Anna refuses to accept the roles traditionally imposed on women by society. She has to come up with different roles such as the role of the writer, the role of a Communist activist, the role of the working mother and that of a mistress. Having to combine all these roles in the class ridden British post war society brings about identity problems. Anna's "source of self-respect was that she had not – as she put it – given up and crawled into safety somewhere. Into a safe marriage."[11]

By describing troubled relationships throughout the novel the author shows women's dissatisfaction with men.[12] *The Golden Notebook* talks about men's sexual inadequacies, about Anna's and Molly's lovers who are inept and emotionally detached and it shows the devastating effect which such men have on women's lives. What is especially outstanding in this novel is that it discusses openly female sexuality f. e. Ella compares vaginal and clitoral orgasm.[13]

---

[5] Cf. Stern, Frederick C.: Politics and The Golden Notebook. In: Kaplan, p. 38-41;
Cf. Taylor, Jenny: Notebook/memoirs/archives. Reading and Rereading Doris Lessing.Routeledge & Kegan Paul, Boston, 1982, p. 43f.;
Cf. McCrindle, Jean: Reading The Golden Notebook in 1962. In: Taylor, Jenny:
Notebook/memoirs/archives. Reading and Rereading Doris Lessing.Routeledge & Kegan Paul, Boston, 1982, p. 52
[6] Lessing, Doris: The Golden Notebook. Paladin Grafton Books, London Glasgow, 1990, p. 8
[7] Lessing, Doris: The Golden Notebook, p. 10
[8] Cf. Sprague, Claire: In Pursuit of Doris Lessing. Nine Nations Reading. The Macmillan Press, London, 1990, p. 9 and Cf. Fahim, S. Shadia: Doris Lessing, p. 59f.
[9] Lessing, Doris: The Golden Notebook. p. 26
[10] ibid, p. 59
[11] ibid, p. 36
[12] Cf. Cheng, Yuan-Jung: Heralds of the Postmodern, p 77ff.
Cf. Seiler-Franklin, Carol: Women in the fiction of Margaret Drabble. Doris Lessing, and Iris Murdoch. Peter Lang, Bern, 1979, p. 131f.;
Cf. Fahim, S Shadia: Doris Lessing, p 61f.
[13] Cf Taylor, Jenny: Notebook/memoirs/archives, p. 52 and Cf. Seiler-Franklin.Carol: Women in the fiction, p. 133

Another important characteristic feature which slips into Lessing's novel repeatedly is the new way of treating psychological problems. Anna undergoes repeatedly psychotherapy and sees her psychotherapist nicknamed "Mother Sugar". In the course of her treatment the interpretation of her dreams is very important, which shows us the influence of Freud and especially of C.G. Jung with his theory of **psychoanalysis**.[14]

A central theme in *The Golden Notebook* are Anna's doubts about the **meaningfulness of literature** because - as she states herself - in a world which "is so chaotic, art is irrelevant"[15]. Anna – cannot support the chaos and meaninglessness and therefore she wants to write a "book powered with an intellectual or moral passion strong enough to create order, to create a new way of looking at life "[16]. But first she has to overcome her writer's block which makes her doubt about the ability of language to convey reality clearly because "the real experience can't be described"[17].[18]

The form and an interpretation:

Doris Lessing is not a narrator in the traditional sense. She wanted to leave behind the form of the conventional realistic novel. Therefore she chose such an extraordinary construction perhaps a kind of parody of conventional realistic novel.

The skeleton is the short novel "Free Women" which could stand for itself and is some kind of frame story which is divided into five sections by four notebooks.[19] The notebooks are told by Anna Wulf, the main figure of "Free Women" and each of them focuses on a different aspect of Annas experiences.

The Black Notebook is about Anna's time in South Africa and about her best seller "Frontiers of War".

The Red Notebook reports about Anna's political views and actions and also her attitude towards the Communist Party.[20]

In the Yellow Notebook there are outlines of novels and short stories which should help to digest Anna's experience. This notebook contains "The Shadow of the Third" – a manuscript of a novel about a married man and his mistress. It deals indirectly with Anna's five-year relationship with Michael, which Lessing projects onto Ella and Paul, two fictional characters.[21]

---

[14] Cf. Stern, Frederick C.: Politics and The Golden Notebook. In: Kaplan, p. 44f. and 54f.;
Cf. Fahim, S. Shadia: Doris Lessing, 55f. and p. 63f.
[15] Lessing, Doris: The Golden Notebook, p 57
[16] ibid, p. 76
[17] ibid, p. 549
[18] Cf. Sprague, Claire: In Pursuit of Doris Lessing, p. 66f.;
Cf. Cheng, Yuan-Jung: Heralds of the Postmodern, p. 88
Cf. Seiler-Franklin, Carol: Women in the fiction, p. 128f.
Cf. Fahim, S. Shadia: Doris Lessing,, p. 57f.
[19] Cf. Lessing, Doris: The Golden Notebook, p. 7
[20] Cf. Fahim, S. Shadia: Doris Lessing,, p. 57ff
[21] Cf. Fahim, S. Shadia: Doris Lessing,, p 60ff

The form of the novel is of immense importance [22] and underlines and reflects the novel's meaning as Doris Lessing herself commented in the preface to her novel " ...my major aim was to shape a book which would make its own comment about the conventional novel, ... a wordless statement: to talk through the way it was shaped..."[23].

Anna's split personality corresponds to the formal fragmentation (in 4 notebooks) and to the social and political chaos in the world. She writes these notebooks to analyse her experience and her inner state of mind and to make order of her experiences by dividing her life into four different sections. Her personality is imbalanced because she sees each aspect of her life separately.[24] Because of this fragmented perception her reality is distorted. She looks for an equilibrium within her personality. This can only be achieved by giving up writing in her notebooks which she closes one after the other with a double black line and by beginning a new one- *The Golden Notebook*, which gives the novel its title. In bringing together her different experiences ("all of myself in one book"[25]) a certain unity comes into existence which helps to regulate her imbalance in her consciousness and leads her to a more comprehensive understanding of reality.

This turning point in her life has been brought about by Michael breaking up the relationship and the painful but very intense affair with Saul Green which was following. When the pressures become unbearable she has a breakdown. Saul being in the same mental state helps her to regain her inner stability.[26] She realizes that destruction is not only outside in the world but also in her inner self what proves the dream about destruction which Anna named "joy in spite"[27].

"I was in a dream with another person... I understood that this terrible malicious force was in that person who was a friend... a person who had the power to move me... if the element is... inside another human being, then it can only mean it is loose in me also, or can only too easily be evoked.[28]"

Based on this experience she can build up a new relation to reality. As soon as she has come over her past and her personal crisis she has overcome her writer's block. On Paul / Saul's advice she starts writing a new novel called "Free Women" which describes Anna's alienation from her self and thus

[22] Cf. Danzinger, Marie A.: Text/Countertext. Postmodern Paranoia in Samuel Beckett, Doris Lessing, and Philip Roth. Peter Lang Verlag, New York, 1996, p. 63f. and Cf. Fahim, S. Shadia: Doris Lessing, p. 52
[23] Lessing, Doris: The Golden Notebook, p. 13
[24] Cf. Fahim, S. Shadia: Doris Lessing, p 57f.
[25] Lessing, Doris: The Golden Notebook, p. 528
[26] Cf. Danzinger, Marie A.: Text/Countertext, p. 71f. and Cf. Seiler-Franklin, Carol: Women in the fiction, p. 138f
[27] Lessing, Doris: The Golden Notebook, p. 419
[28] ibid, p. 420f.

summons up the notebooks. It is identic with the frame story "Free Women" of Lessing's novel "*The Golden Notebook*".

In Lessing's novel a very complex time scheme can be noted. Therefore I found it impossible to draw a structure diagram. The outlay of the contents, which I put in the handout shows the rough structure of the novel.

The notebooks are written over the same period of time- between 1950 and 1957. But the author does not necessarily stick to a chronological order of the events in these notebooks because she sometimes changes the sequence of events. In the Red Notebook the joining of the Communist Party is even recorded within entries from Anna's decision to leave it.

The events recorded in the Black Notebook are very often disconnected and there are from time to time flashbacks into the past to show how Anna revives certain past experience. Some entries are broken off in one notebook – for example a few years are totally left out in the Blue Notebook but they can be followed in the other notebooks.

In addition to this certain sequences of Anna's life are reviewed a number of times but from different perspectives.

Choosing this time scheme the author makes the linear reading of the novel impossible and the reader is forced to reconstruct Anna's life by connecting parts to parts.[29]

Anna Wulf being a writer herself takes the role of Doris Lessing and comments instead of her.

In the notebooks Anna Wulf tells her experience in the first person[30] whereas the same Anna Wulf tells her life in the third-person[31] in the novel "Free Women". Thus Lessing removes the distinction between fiction and truth.

"...the novel-within-a-novel technique, goes beyond that truth/fiction issue, and focuses on the very essence of the balancing of different levels of perception which is the basic theme of *The Golden Notebook*"[32].

The "frame-novel" and the notebooks are not identical but they enrich each other for example the incident with Tommy, who tried to shoot himself, is described in the novel but never mentioned in the notebooks.

Of course a short treatment of this hefty about 600 pages long tome cannot accommodate all possible facets. I hope I could give you an overview on this complex novel which is really worth reading.

---

[29] Cf. Fahim, S Shadia Doris Lessing, p. 78f.

[30] Cf. Tiger, Virginia: Illusions of Actuality· First-Person Pronoun in The Golden Notebook. In: Kaplan. Carey/Rose, Ellen Cronan: Approaches to Teaching Lessing's The Golden Notebook. The Modern Language Association of America, New York, 1989, p. 101-108

[31] Cf. Danzinger, Marie A.: Text/Countertext. p. 61f.

[32] Fahim, S. Shadia: Doris Lessing, p. 80

The Golden Notebook by Doris Lessing

The Golden Notebook was published in 1962 and is one of the best known of
Doris Lessing's novels.

Summary:
The central figure of *"The Golden Notebook"* is Anna Wulf, a writer from
South Africa, living in London. During World War II Anna marries a German
refugee Max but divorces and then emigrates to London with her daughter
Janet. She has a long love affair with Michael and an intense friendship with
Molly.
Being about thirty Anna is in a life crises, disillusioned by communist politics
under Stalin, doubting herself and her literary career. Therefore she needs the
treatment of a psychotherapist. To get things straightened out with herself she
deals with them in four independent notebooks, each one has a different
colour.

Sociopolitical context and main ideas:
As the following part will prove *The Golden Notebook* shows features of a
political novel as well as characteristics of a novel of ideas and has, besides
this, various autobiographic traces.
Racism is not a central topic in *The Golden Notebook* but the problem is
mentioned when the protagonist, Anna, talks about her successful novel
"Frontiers of War" which concerns race relations and forbidden love in
southern Africa.
Doris Lessing escaped from this colonial society to London like Anna. There
she was confronted with the effects of the Cold War in the 1950s which are
mentioned in the novel just as the dangers of nuclear threats are.
Doris Lessing and Anna were both deeply involved in **politics** and together
with most of their friends they became members of the Communist Party. But
trials and atrocities in the Soviet Union and other communist countries or
revelations about Stalin's crimes made them develop a feeling of doubt and
disappointment towards **Communism** which was why they broke with
communism.
Besides this *The Golden Notebook* is about **feminism**. Although Lessing
herself claimed in the preface to the book: "This novel was not a trumpet for
Women's Liberation...", her friends called it "a tract about the sex war".
Anna and Doris Lessing being divorced with a child symbolize "a completely
new type of woman" because they "lead what is known as free lives, that is,
lives like men."
Anna refuses to accept the roles traditionally imposed on women by society.
By describing troubled relationships throughout the novel the author shows
women's dissatisfaction with men.

Another important characteristic feature which slips into Lessing's novel repeatedly is the new way of treating psychological problems. Anna undergoes repeatedly psychotherapy and sees her psychotherapist nicknamed "Mother Sugar". In the course of her treatment the interpretation of her dreams is very important which shows us the influence of Freud and especially of C.G. Jung with his theory of **psychoanalysis**.

A central theme in *The Golden Notebook* are Anna's doubts about the meaningfulness of **literature**.

Structure, time scheme and interpretation (chart of the action):

Doris Lessing wanted to leave behind the form of the conventional realistic novel. Therefore she chose such an extraordinary construction.

The skeleton is the short novel "Free Women" which could stand for itself and is some kind of frame story which is divided into five sections by four notebooks. The notebooks are told by Anna Wulf the main figure of Free Women (each notebook focusing on a different kind of experience).

The Black Notebook is about Anna's time in South Africa and about her best seller "Frontiers of War".

The Red Notebook reports about Anna's political views and her attitudes towards the Communist Party.

The Yellow Notebook contains "The Shadow of the Third" – a manuscript of a novel about a married man and his mistress. It deals indirectly with Anna's five-year relationship with Michael which Lessing projects onto Ella and Paul two fictional characters.

The form of the novel is of immense importance and underlines and reflects the novel's meaning.

Anna's split personality corresponds to the formal fragmentation. The protagonist is imbalanced because she sees each aspect of her life separately. She looks for an equilibrium within her personality. This can only be achieved by giving up writing in her notebooks and by beginning a new one- *The Golden Notebook*, which gives the novel its title. In bringing together her different experiences a certain unity comes into existence which helps to regulate her imbalance in her consciousness.

This turning point in her life has been brought about by the painful but very intense affair with Saul Green. Saul being in the same mental state helps her to regain her personality and individual stability. Based on this experience she can build up a new relation to reality. As soon as she has got over her personal crisis then she has overcome her writer's block.

In Lessing's novel a very complex time scheme can be noted.

The notebooks are written over the same period of time- between 1950 and 1957. But the author does not necessarily stick to a chronological order of the events in these notebooks because she sometimes changes the sequence of events. (Futher details **p. 3f.**)

Anna Wulf being a writer herself takes the role of Doris Lessing and comments instead of her.

In the notebooks Anna Wulf tells her experience in the first person whereas the same Anna Wulf tells her life in the third-person in the novel "Free Women". Thus Lessing removes the distinction between fiction and truth.

Bibliography:

- Lessing, Doris: The Golden Notebook. Paladin Grafton Books, London Glasgow, 1990
- Fahim, S. Shadia: Doris Lessing. Sufi Equilibrium and the Form of the Novel. St. Matin's Press, New York, 1994
- Cheng, Yuan-Jung: Heralds of the Postmodern. Madness and Fiction in Conrad, Woolf, and Lessing. Peter Lang, New York, 1999
- Taylor, Jenny: Notebooks/memoirs/archives. Reading and Rereading Doris Lessing. Routledge & Kegan Paul, Boston, 1982
- Danziger, Marie A.: Text/Countertext. Postmodern Paranoia in Samuel Beckett, Doris Lessing, and Philip Roth. Peter Lang, New York , 1996
- Sprague, Claire: In Pursuit of Doris Lessing. Nine Nations Reading. The Macmillan Press, London, 1990
- Kaplan, Carey/Rose, Ellen Cronan: Approaches to Teaching Lessing's The Golden Notebook. The Modern Language Association of America, New York, 1989
- Seiler-Franklin, Carol: Women in the fiction of Margaret Drabble, Doris Lessing, and Iris Murdoch. Peter Lang, Bern, 1979

Structure of the novel:

"The two women were alone in the London flat"

Summer 1957-Anna re-meets Molly

about Molly's husband Richard, his wife Marion, their unhappy marriage

flashback: how Molly and Richard met

Molly occupations: dancing, drawing lessons, actress, journalist

Molly's son (Tommy), Richard's attempts to find a constructive place for him

first doubts about communism.

Flashback: when Anna met Michael (lived with him from 1949-1954)

1951 ??? Anna and agent discussing the making of a film **"Frontiers of War"**

1952 discussion about cast for this film

1953 Memories about African time ...about RAF

Novel Reviews

Flashback: end of African period after the war, about weekends with communist group (Paul, Jimmy, Ted, George, Willy, Maryrose...)

January 1950 ...February 1950....Communist Party

August 1951 Michael dropped in

September 15th Hungarian Trial

January 3rd 1952 friends of Michael hanged in Prague, Rosenbergs electrocuted

Stalin's death

Julia and Ella working for a women's magazine

Ella writing novel about suicide

Ella's son Michael...

party at Dr. West's house...

Ella about her ex-husband George

About her affair with Paul (a married doctor) - does not want to abandon his wife and his two children...leaves Ella

looking at Ella's affair with Paul Anna realizes what has happened to her and Michael

Ella's statements about orgasm

Commentary to the sociogram:

Now I want to have a quick look at the different characters of this novel and show how they interrelate.

I am going to start with the characters of "The Shadow of the Third" a mise-en-abyme novel written into the Yellow notebook. [1]

Ella is the divorced wife of **George**, with whom she has a son called **Michael**. She has an intense affair with the married physician **Paul** Tanner and an enriching friendship with **Julia**. They are all counterparts of the characters of *The Golden Notebook* itself.

We hear about **Anna**'s husband **Max**, leader of the political group in Africa, a cold and doctrinaire German refugee, whom she divorced after the war and with whom she had a daughter, called **Janet**.

Janet leaves for boarding school when she is twelve. (She gave Anna's life an outer shape and afterwards "An Anna is coming to life that died when Janet was born.")

Like Ella, Anna has a close relationship with a woman friend, **Molly**. [2]

And she has two lovers, first **Michael**, and then **Saul Green**.

When Anna reflects on the events that took place in Africa (at the Mashopi Hotel...) we hear about the members of the left-wing political group made up of English airman and local white activists in Africa during World War II... like **Paul, Willy, Maryrose**...

Molly's ex-husband **Richard** is a failure in private life, but a mogul of British industry. He is unhappily married, to **Marion**, who has drinking problems and is rejected by Richard.

Tommy, Richard's son from his first marriage to Molly, suffers from depression and decided to become a conscientious objector. He blinds himself when trying to shoot himself. After his attempted suicide he moves in with his step-mother, Marion.

Anna begins a brief affair with the American, **Saul** (called **Milt** in "Free Women 5").

Saul is an American drop-out with several nervous breakdowns behind him. Anna takes over his emotions, goes "right inside his craziness". Anna presents her Golden Notebook to Saul with the first sentence of his novel. [3]

At the point Saul and Anna state "we can't either of us ever go lower than that" they are able to start at the beginning ... and then return to sanity.

Then Saul sees himself and Anna as part of the "team that haven't given in".

[1] Cf. Danzinger, Marie Text/Countertext. Postmodern Paranoia in Samuel Beckett, Doris Lessing, and Philip Roth Peter Lang, New York , 1996, p. 6

[2] Cf. Seiler-Franklin, Carol: Women in the fiction of Margaret Drabble, Doris Lessing, and Iris Murdoch Peter Lang, Bern, 1979, p. 140f.

[3] Cf Ibid, p 138f

Stylistic Analysis:

It was impossible for me to choose one "key" text extract in order to show characteristic stylistic features of this novel. Doris Lessing has used different kinds of writing and various styles.

Styles change when she refers to other works of fiction like "Frontiers of War" or "The Shadow of the Third" or Saul Green's novel about the Algerian soldier or when she writes various numbered ideas for stories and novels. There are letters, book reviews, newspaper clippings all in different styles.

"A description of her meeting with Joyce, as recorded in the Red Notebook, reveals that pattern in epitome: *'this evening had dinner with Joyce, New Statesman circles, and she started to attack Soviet Union. Instantly I found myself doing that automatic-defence-of-Soviet-Union act, which I can't stand when other people do it. She went on; I went on. For her, she was in the presence of a communist so she started on certain clichés. I returned them. Twice tried to break the thing, start on a different level, failed – the atmosphere prickling with hostility. '*"

Especially in the blue notebook where she gives detailed accounts of Anna's life we are confronted with a language typical of diary entries:
"*Jan. 7th, 1950. ... Country house. Charming conventional wife. Three delightful little boys. ...Richard at home for week-ends, bringing business guests, etc. The local gentry.*"

Talking about the Communist Party or the activities for it she uses typical political jargon.
"*It's all right, comrades, we are going to lose our deposit, we aren't going to win enough votes to split the Labour.*"

And there is the language of feminists:
"*You bring out all this stuff, as if it were the last revelation from some kind of oracle. I bet you talk about sex when you're alone with a popsy. So why put on this club-man's act just because there are two of us?*"

And the language of psychotherapists:
"*The things that are important in life creep up on one unawares, one doesn't expect them, one hasn't given them shape in one's mind. One recognizes them...*"

Often there are only words used to write down certain associations:
"*Men. Women. Bound. Free. Good. Bad. Yes. No. Capitalism . Socialism. Sex. Love...*"

sociogram 1

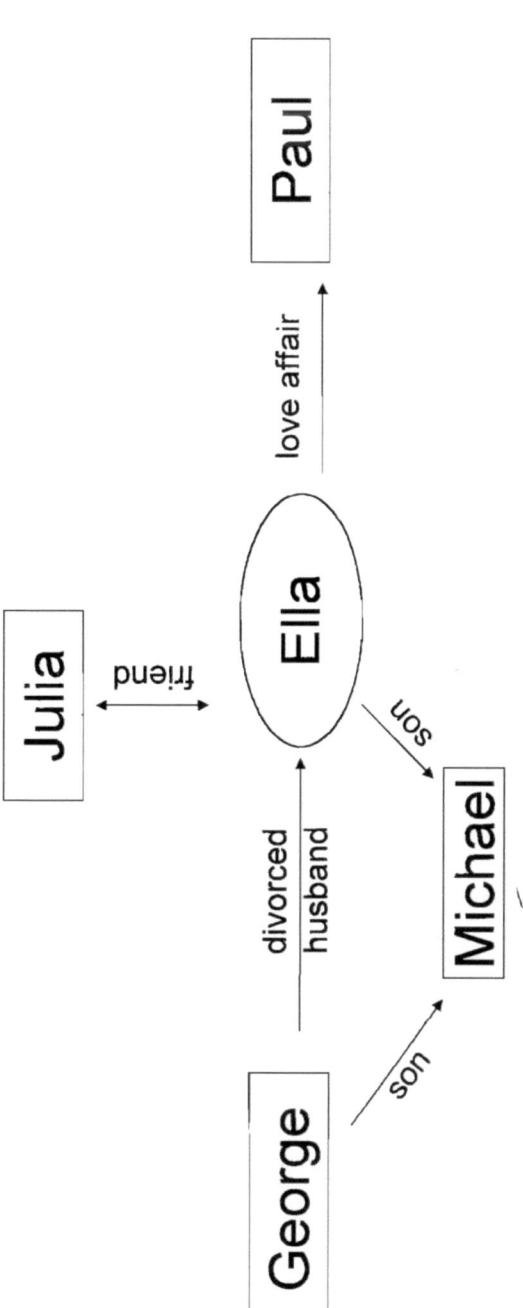